THE 40-MINUTE TEMPEST

KING RAM

T0262446

for Annita

THE 40-MINUTE TEMPEST

Lesley Ross

(freely adapted from *The Tempest* by William Shakespeare)

KING RAM AND THE TARTAN SNOW BABY

Lesley Ross
(Book and Lyrics)

James Williams
(Original Music)

(based on *King Lear* by William Shakespeare)

OBERON BOOKS

LONDON

First published in 2002 by Oberon Books Ltd.
521 Caledonian Road, London N7 9RH
Tel: +44 (0) 20 7607 3637 / Fax: +44 (0) 20 7607 3629
e-mail: info@oberonbooks.com
www.oberonbooks.com

PB ISBN: 978-1-84002-313-8
E ISBN: 978-1-84943-840-7

Contents

THE 40-MINUTE TEMPEST

for performance to 6 – 11 year-olds and older

NT Education

The 40-Minute Tempest was commissioned by the National Theatre's Education Department as part of the extensive Primary Shakespeare Programme, the thrust of which is to explore a classic text through creative, practical work with artists in school as well as seeing a professional production. Primary Shakespeare aims to improve literacy and oracy skills for children at Key Stage 2 by participating in drama, design, writing and movement training.

This script of *The 40-Minute Tempest* was developed through the writer's close collaboration with the director and designer.

For more information about primary school links to the National Theatre visit www.nationaltheatre.org.uk.

Characters

Actor One

PROSPERO
Voice of Caliban
STEPHANO
Voice of Sebastian
Voices of Sailors

Actor Two

ARIEL
Voice of Ariel
MIRANDA
FERDINAND
TRINCULO
Voice of Antonio
Voices of Sailors

Caliban is always represented by a puppet.

Ariel can be represented by various forms. Glove puppet, flying puppet on a stick, puppet in a hat, large puppet, then also as human with puppet like features, a harpy puppet. As the play progresses, though, she becomes more and more human. When she is set free she is totally human.

Alonso, Sebastian, Antonio and Gonzalo are represented by small puppets.

The 40-Minute Tempest was commissioned by The Royal National Theatre and was first performed there on 7 May 2002, with the following cast:

PROSPERO, Stewart C Scudamore

ARIEL, Laura Rees

Director, Rebecca Gould

Designer, Caroline Jones

Producer, Rachel Dickinson

Assistant Director, Lisa Spirling

Puppetry Consultant, Mervyn Millar

Music, Ansuman Biswas

Stage Manager, Louise Balhatchet

Some of the design elements set out in this script are as a result of a collaboration process, which happened prior to the first performance.

ACT ONE

On stage a tree. Suspended from the tree is PROSPERO's cloak. Near this a table, as a representation of the island. The pieces of the table are perhaps black and white, like that of a chessboard. Pages of manuscript, neatly set in piles, adorn the stage. In a pre-show workshop, three children have been selected to represent ANTONIO, SEBASTIAN and ALONSO (King of Naples). They have been given a hat or headdress that exactly matches puppets used later in the performance. One of the teachers or adults has been selected to wear GONZALO's hat and will represent him, as he is older than the others. Music plays as PROSPERO enters. He carries a small puppet, which he gently places on the table. He looks around him.

PROSPERO: Shhh. Shhh. (*He smiles. He lifts his hand and blows magic dust in the air.*) Listen. Spirits. Inhabitants of this isle. For I would like to tell you a tale of two brothers. Of betrayal. (*He lifts up the small puppet.*) Look, spirits. Here stands the Duke of Milan. Prospero. A man who loved books. Magic books. A man, who so loved the study of his books, he let his brother rule his Kingdom. Look at him, spirits. And I will tell you how neglect of his people led him to this island of dreams. Of spirits. Of magic. (*Sets puppet at the back of stage.*) Come away, servant, come; I'm ready now. Approach, my Ariel. Come!

We hear the voice of ARIEL.

ARIEL: All hail, great master, grave sir, hail! I come
  To answer thy best pleasure; be't to fly
  To swim, to dive into the fire, to ride
  On the curled clouds. To thy strong bidding task
  Ariel and all his quality.

PROSPERO: That's my spirit. Soon you will be free. (*To audience.*) But now, let us meet Prospero's brother. For

11

it is time to tell their tale, these brothers. (*He approaches the child who has been given ANTONIO's hat/headdress.*) See, spirits, see the brother that Prospero loved. (*To another child.*) Are you listening, spirit? This is a tale of great sadness. And greater magic yet to come. Yes, and this is Antonio. Prospero's brother. A brother who desired to become the Duke of Milan. Who believed he should be the Duke. And so, like the ivy that grips the walls of an ancient castle, took hold of his brother's power. While Prospero continued to study his magic books. Unaware of the danger he was in. Unaware that Antonio was plotting against him. Plotting with Prospero's enemies. There they are. (*Pointing out the two children with the relevant crown/head dress.*) The King of Naples and his brother, Sebastian. Here sits the King of Naples. Here sits his brother. And with their army these two helped Antonio overthrow the Duke Prospero, and so Antonio became The Duke of Milan. But what became of Prospero? And what became of his only child and heir? His baby daughter. His darling child. His darling Miranda. Were they slaughtered? Killed? No, spirits. There was no bloody business. (*He takes the cloak from the tree.*) No murder. Instead these three men sent Prospero and his daughter out to sea. In a ship even the rats were afraid to travel in. (*PROSPERO is now wearing the cloak. Music starts to swell.*) And I am that same Prospero, now ruler of this island.

ARIEL enters, carrying a ship. Inside the ship are small puppet representations of ANTONIO, ALONSO, SEBASTIAN and GONZALO.

And these three men now find themselves on a ship. (*Points.*) That ship. That ship that Fortune has brought to my island. And I am now more powerful than I have ever been. I know of the magic that is found outside the realm of man! Magic books filled with a magic rich in the spirit world! Spirits. Let the Tempest begin!

Music. There is a tempest, created by the children, as ARIEL passes through them with the ship. They create the waves, the noises, learnt in a pre-show workshop. They may also have some inflatable thunderclouds passing through them. On a recording we hear the lines from Act 1 Scene 1 line 54 'Mercy on us!' to 56 'We split, we split, we split!' repeated on sound recording as the tempest happens. PROSPERO helps orchestrate the children as the ship passes amongst them culminating with him laying his cloak on the floor. ARIEL brings the boat to the magic cloak and pours the puppet men onto the material, and hangs the ship on the tree. PROSPERO calms the storm.

Hast thou, spirit, performed to point the tempest
That I bade thee?

ARIEL: To every article.

PROSPERO: My brave spirit!

ARIEL: All
Plunged in the foaming brine and quit the vessel,
Then all a-fire with me, the king's son Ferdinand,
Was the first man that leaped; cried: 'Hell is empty!'
(*Runs behind PROSPERO's cloak.*)

PROSPERO: Ariel, thy charge
Exactly is performed; but there's more work.

ARIEL has changed into MIRANDA and runs on.

And so to my daughter, Miranda.

MIRANDA: If by your art, my dearest father, you have
Put the wild waters in this roar, allay them.
The sky it seems would pour down stinking pitch,
But that the sea, mounting to th'welkin's cheek,
Dashes the fire out!

PROSPERO: Child, the storm has passed. The ship is

safely at harbour.

MIRANDA: O I have suffered
With those that I saw suffer!

PROSPERO: No child, it was a trick of the night.

MIRANDA: Pour souls, they perished.

PROSPERO: No more amazement. Tell your piteous heart
There's no harm done.

MIRANDA: O Woe the day.

PROSPERO: No harm. I have done nothing but in care
of thee. Sssh. For now, the storm has past (*He calms the
noise of the sea.*) And the night is over (*He gently places the
puppets on the table so that she can see them.*) See, the magic
is done. (*The music fades.*) And no one was harmed. I
promise you.

MIRANDA: No one was harmed?

PROSPERO: No child. They have all survived the storm.

MIRANDA: But, how did *we* survive, Father? How did we
survive the storms that brought *us* here?

PROSPERO: Did you not listen when I told you the story
of our coming here?

MIRANDA: Oh, I listened, Father. With all my heart. But
tell me once more the things that kept us safe. For I am
so full of fear for those who I saw drowning.

PROSPERO: There are none drowned, my dearest child.

MIRANDA: Please father, calm me like you did the storm.
Tell me what kept us alive when they threw us into that
rotting ship.

PROSPERO: Very well, my angel. Three things helped us
stay alive.

MIRANDA: Three things helped us stay alive.

PROSPERO: Yes.

MIRANDA: (*Runs and looks out into the distance.*) One?

PROSPERO: Your sweet face kept my spirits up. You who were little more than three years old.

MIRANDA: (*Looks into the past.*) My sweet face. And the second thing?

PROSPERO: The Gods shined down on us and brought us safely to this island.

MIRANDA: Yes. The kindness of the Gods. And the third?

PROSPERO: (*He shows her the puppet of an old man.*) My dear friend Gonzalo, who gave us clothes and food, and my beloved magical books.

MIRANDA: (*Kissing the puppet.*) One day I will kiss this hand for real. And thank him with all my heart.

PROSPERO: But enough now. (*Hypnotises her.*) Sleep. No more questions. Sleep! (*She falls asleep and he is wearing his cloak, standing in front of her.*) Ariel? Ariel? Approach, my Ariel. Come!

ARIEL: (*Appearing as puppet in cloak.*)
Is there more toil? Since thou dost give me pains
Let me remember thee what thou hast promised.

PROSPERO: What is't thou canst demand?

ARIEL: My liberty.

PROSPERO: Before time be out? No more.

ARIEL turns her head away from PROSPERO.

PROSPERO: (*Stroking ARIEL.*) And after two days I will discharge thee.

ARIEL: (*Returning.*) That's my noble master! What shall I
    do?
    Say what? What shall I do?

PROSPERO: Are they, Ariel, safe?

ARIEL: (*As puppet.*) Not a hair perished;
    In troops I have dispersed them 'bout the isle.
    The king's son have I landed by himself.

PROSPERO: Go make thyself
    Like to a nymph of the sea. Be invisible
    To every eyeball else. Go take this shape!

The puppet disappears.

And now, Miranda, wake up. Come, child, wake up, for
it is time we made a visit to Caliban.

PROSPERO goes to collect CALIBAN.

MIRANDA: No, Father. I don't want to see that creature
    any more.

PROSPERO: And yet, as it is, we can hardly miss him. For
    he fetches in our wood, and does many other things that
    help us. Caliban! Caliban!

CALIBAN's head appears. He looks around the stage.
He is manipulated by PROSPERO.

CALIBAN: As wicked dew as e'er my mother brushed
    With raven's feather from unwholesome fen
    Drop on you both! A south-west wind blow on ye
    And blister ye all over!

MIRANDA: For this, be sure, tonight thou shalt have
    cramps!

CALIBAN: This island's mine! By Sycorax my mother
    Which thou tak'st from me. When thou cam'st first
    Thou strok'st me and made much of me: wouldst give

me
Water with berries in't. And then I loved thee.
Cursed be I that did so! (*Starts to exit.*) All the charms
Of Sycorax – toads, beetles, bats – light on you!
For I am all the subjects that you have,
Which first was mine own king; and here you sty me
In this hard rock, whiles you do keep from me
The rest o'th'island.

MIRANDA: Thou most lying slave,
Being capable of all ill! I pitied thee,
Took pains to make thee speak, taught thee each hour
One thing or other. But thy vile race, savage –
Though thou didst learn – had that in't which good natures
Could not abide to be with; therefore was thou
Deservedly confined into this rock.

CALIBAN: O ho, O ho! The red plague rid you for
learning me your language! (*He runs at her.*)

MIRANDA: (*Running off.*) Aaaah!

PROSPERO: Hag seed, hence! (*Returning CALIBAN.*) And
so the monster Caliban returns to his cave. But wait
spirits. Who comes now? It is Ferdinand. Son to the
King of Naples. I'll make myself invisible.

FERDINAND enters.

ARIEL'S VOICE: (*Recorded.*)
Come into these yellow sands
And then take hands
Hark, hark
The watch dogs bark!
Bow, wow, bow, wow
Hark, hark, I hear
Cry cock a diddle dow!

FERDINAND: Where should this music be? I'th'air, or th'earth?
It sounds no more; and sure it waits upon

Some god o'th'island. Sitting on a bank,
Weeping again the king my father's wrack,
This music crept by me upon the waters.

There is a music change.

*PROSPERO watches FERDINAND as MIRANDA's
face appears.*

FERDINAND: But look. Look at this. This face floating
in the air. Look at this thing of wonder. Oh wondrous
beauty. Is this a dream or does this beauty live,
somewhere here upon the isle?

PROSPERO: See now the vision, Ferdinand, of your
newfound Lord.

FERDINAND: And now I see the picture of an old man,
who holds my angel and yet keeps me from her.

PROSPERO: No picture. Just a man. Just a tired old man.

FERDINAND: You understand English! Thank heavens!
Are you the ruler of this island?

PROSPERO: Yes, I am the ruler here. And this is my
daughter.

FERDINAND: She's beautiful, sir.

PROSPERO: Perhaps.

FERDINAND: No sir, that is the face of true beauty. I
would go so far as to say that is the most beautiful face I
have ever seen. This very face that I see facing me.

PROSPERO: And what business do you have with this
face? These two eyes? These lips? This nose?

FERDINAND: If she lives, sir, if she is free, then I'll make
her the Queen of Naples.

PROSPERO: How wonderful. And how are you to do

this? Are you the King of Naples?

FERDINAND: Pardon, sir, but that *is* who I am. It's what I do. What I live for now. For I am the son of the King that was, and I have seen him drowned. So therefore I am now the King.

PROSPERO: Really? I think perhaps you are nothing but a spy, sent here to take this island from me.

FERDINAND: No, sir, I promise. I am the King of Naples. It's who I am. All I live for now.

PROSPERO: So why don't I believe you? Why do I think you are either a spy or a traitor?

FERDINAND: I am not a traitor.

PROSPERO: Come, follow me.

FERDINAND: No. I will not!

PROSPERO: No?

FERDINAND: No!

He draws and PROSPERO uses magic to stop him from moving. Three times he tries to attack PROSPERO and three times he is thrown back. The third time he falls to the floor.

PROSPERO: Put up thy sword, traitor?
I'll manacle thy neck and feet together
Sea water shalt thou drink.

The weapon drops.

Follow!
For I can here disarm thee with a stick
And make thy weapon drop.

FERDINAND: You are using some magic that I don't

know, and so I'll follow you. But let me see your
daughter's face and whatever prison you have for me
shall be nothing more than a palace.

PROSPERO: Come, go in, I have work enough for you.

FERDINAND goes behind the cloak.

And so, spirits, my plan takes shape. But come, brave
spirit, where have you gone? My magic continues. And
grows stronger. It works. Come on!

ARIEL appears as puppet in the cloak.

Thou hast done well, fine Ariel. Thou shalt be as free
As mountain winds, but then exactly do
All points of my command. To the syllable.

ARIEL disappears.

End of Act One.

ACT TWO

PROSPERO: And so, spirits. What news of these treacherous few? (*He draws attention to the puppets on the table.*) Alonso, Sebastian and Antonio. (*He blows magic dust over th*em.) I know they have come to no harm. For though this island seem to be a desert, uninhabitable, and almost inaccessible – yet the air breathes upon us most sweetly. Here is everything advantageous to life. (*Approaches teacher.*) And so my friend Gonzalo will be safe.

Music. ARIEL appears as a puppet on a large fibre-glass rod. This could be perhaps just her face. She flies around the audience. And arrives on or near the head of PROSPERO.

PROSPERO: Ah, there you are spirit. What news of the King of Naples?

ARIEL flies and hovers over the boy who is ALONSO. She returns to PROSPERO's hand.

I see. He sleeps, dreaming of his son. And what of Gonzalo? My dear old friend.

ARIEL flies and hovers over the teacher who is GONZALO.

Also asleep?

ARIEL flies around the audience and comes to rest on the shoulder of PROSPERO.

PROSPERO: That's my fine spirit. And what of my brother, Antonio? And Sebastian, brother to the King of Naples. Are they asleep too? No? Come spirits, lets listen to what they are saying. Magic winds, fill our ears with magic voices. So we may know their thoughts, see their actions, hear their words.

ARIEL hovers over ANTONIO.

ANTONIO: (*Recorded voice.*) What might, worthy Sebastian, O, what might?

PROSPERO: My brother. Antonio.

ANTONIO: (*Recorded voice.*) My strong imagination sees a crown
Dropping upon thy head.

PROSPERO: My brother, plotting with the King's brother. Persuading him to take the throne from the King of Naples. And now, Ariel, how does Sebastian reply?

ARIEL hovers over SEBASTIAN.

SEBASTIAN: (*Recorded voice.*) As thou got'st Milan, I'll come by Naples.

PROSPERO: Sebastian speaks. The web is spun. He has been persuaded. They are going to kill the King.

SEBASTIAN: (*Recorded voice.*) Draw thy sword!

ARIEL flies to ANTONIO.

ANTONIO: (*Recorded voice.*) Draw together.

PROSPERO: We must wake these sleepers! Before they are murdered.

ANTONIO: (*Recorded voice.*) Then let us both be sudden.

PROSPERO: Spirits! Sing!

ARIEL flies around the children.

ARIEL/SPIRITS: If of life you keep a care
Shake off slumber and beware
Awake, awake!

Music and noise. Possibly percussion from some of the children.

ARIEL exits.

PROSPERO: And so the King and Gonzalo are saved. But what noise is that? Caliban. He is a hideous thing. And yet, sometimes, even his voice springs forth with beauty.

CALIBAN's head appears. He is still a puppet and PROSPERO goes over to manipulate him.

CALIBAN: All the infections that the sun sucks up
On Prosper fall. His spirits hear me and
For every trifle are they set upon me,
Sometime like apes –

Recorded background sounds.

– that mow and chatter at me
And after bite me; then like hedgehogs, which
Lie tumbling in my barefoot way and mount
Their pricks at my footfall. Ouch!

TRINCULO groans.

Lo, now, lo!
Here comes a spirit of his, and to torment me
For bringing wood in slowly. I'll fall flat.

He hides under a sheet or cloak.

PROSPERO leaves him and exits as TRINCULO enters.

There is thunder.

TRINCULO; Nowhere to hide. Nowhere to run. Knowing nobody. I'm cold. I'm hungry. I just wanna go home!! And if I have to walk one more step, I think I…

Thunder.

…can hear thunder again! Please don't rain again. I'm wet enough as it is. You mark my words. As I am Trinculo, so… (*Sees CALIBAN.*) Oh? What the hell is that?

Mmmm? It's a …It's a… Well, I don't know what it is. Is it alive? Is it human? Could it be a fish? Whoa! It smells like a fish. It stinks! No, worse than that. It doesn't stink. It Mings! It mings like the most mingy thing in the world. It's like Maximus Mingimus. No, swear on my life. This Gladiator they forgot to clean up in Rome. After the lions got him. He lay there for the whole Summer. Ming, Ming, Ming! That's where the word Ming comes from. From Maximus Mingimus. Yeah. Swear on my life. In fact, here's something I picked up in the sea. (*Gets out puppet fish head that smells.*) Sniff that. Yeah, well that (*CALIBAN.*) mings worse than this. It'll make me a fortune. Swear on my life. And that's just the way he smells, let alone the way he looks. I mean, look at its legs. Oh my word, they're warm. I guess it must belong to the island. And probably just got hit by one of them there those thunderbolts.

Thunder.

Oh, not again. I can't stand this. I guess I'm gonna have to hide under his…gaberdine! Now, repeat after me. Gaberdine!

AUDIENCE: Gaberdine!

TRINCULO: Ga-Ba-Deen!

AUDIENCE: Ga-Ba-Deen!

TRINCULO: See, no matter how you say it, Gaberdine is not as effective as the word cloak. Or blanket, even. See, blanket is a blanket word; covers everything. Here, move over you.

Enter STEPHANO, singing.

STEPHANO: Sailing's no longer the life for me
I shall have nothing to do with sea
Soldiers know nothing of agony

For like it not
When you're in a spot…

Stephano doesn't like this song. You see, I like to drink. No, I do. (*Sniffs.*) What you looking at? What's your favourite song? Well, Stephano doesn't like that either. I like to drink. No, I do.

TRINCULO: Oh!!

STEPHANO: (*To child.*) Was that you? Yeah, well, I don't like that noise you're making. Wanna swig some of this? (*Pulls it away.*) Haaah!

TRINCULO: Oh!!

STEPHANO: What is it now? (*Looks.*) See that? That's got four legs. No, it does. See one, two, three… eight. No, four. (*Bends over CALIBAN and lifts his head.*)

CALIBAN: Do not torment me! Please!

STEPHANO: See that. That's a monster. A monster that speaks English. I can make a fortune with that. No, I can. But he's not a happy monster. (*To child.*) Want some of this? (*Pulls bottle away.*) Haaa! This is just for me and my monster now. No, it is. Now, let's see if he wants some of my liquor. There you go, monster. Have some of that.

TRINCULO: I know that voice.

STEPHANO: Oh my word. Now its bum is talking to me. It's got a talking bum. No, it has. Hey, four legs and two voices. And a talking bum! Kings and Queens will pay me a fortune to see this thing. Drink some more, monster! Roll up, roll up, your highness, come and see Stephano and his Monster. See the fabulous Talking Bum!

TRINCULO: Stephano? Is that you?

STEPHANO: His bum knows my name!

TRINCULO: Stephano? If it is you, talk to me, for it's me, Trinculo, your old chum.

STEPHANO: Hey, the Bum says it's my Chum. Eh, that's poetry. No, it is. Well, Trinculo, if that's you come here and have a drink. I like drink. And so does this monster. And so does Trink. Everyone have a drink.

TRINCULO: (*Gets up.*) You're alive! You're alive! I'm saved.

STEPHANO: Trinculo, don't spin me. Or I might (*Nearly sick.*) Over one of these. (*Nearly sick again.*) So sorry.

TRINCULO: How did you escape?

STEPHANO: (*Picking up CALIBAN and giving him drink.*) On a barrel of wine, of course. No, I did. And you?

TRINCULO: Swam. Like a duck. A very hungry duck.

STEPHANO: But not a thirsty one, eh? (*Gives TRINCULO a drink.*) Ah, monster. You like the drink, eh?

CALIBAN nods, drinking.

He does. And there's plenty more drink, too. What's that?

CALIBAN whispers in STEPHANO's ear.

You want me to be your God? Hey, Trinculo. Stephano's a God.

TRINCULO: Yeah. God awful.

STEPHANO: Come, then servant, kiss my bottle. Kiss my feet!

CALIBAN kisses STEPHANO's foot.

He thinks I'm a God.

TRINCULO: He's drunk. He'd think you were Puff the Magic Dragon if you said you were.

STEPHANO: Come, kiss.

TRINCULO: Bonkers, both of them. You know what I mean. Bonkers.

STEPHANO: That's my monster.

CALIBAN's following two speeches and song are pre-recorded.

CALIBAN: I'll show thee the best springs: I'll pluck thee

berries.
I'll fish for thee, and get thee wood enough
Thou wondrous man!

TRINCULO: Absolutely bonkers!

CALIBAN: Farewell, master! Farewell, farewell!
    Catch me if you can
    For Ca-Ca-Caliban
    Has a new master! – Get a new man!
    Freedom, o freedom highday Caliban
    Ban, ban, Caliban
    Oh freedom highday ho!
    Oh freedom high
    Highday for freedom day!

STEPHANO: All together now!

ALL; Catch me if you can
    For Ca-Ca-Caliban
    Has a new master! – Get a new man!
    Freedom, o freedom highday Caliban
    Ban, ban, Caliban
    Oh freedom highday ho!
    Oh freedom high
    Highday for freedom day!

They exit. The music of the song fades into the sound of wood chopping.

End of Act Two.

ACT THREE

MIRANDA enters, hiding from her father. She is carrying a log of wood.

PROSPERO enters.

PROSPERO: Where are you going with that log, Miranda?

Silence.

Helping Ferdinand to do his work?

MIRANDA: It's only one log, father.

PROSPERO: Silly girl. You think so much of him? Why? To most people he is as ugly as Caliban.

MIRANDA: I wish to see no other man than him. I have never met 'most people', Father. Why should I care what they think?

PROSPERO: (*Showing MIRANDA the vision of FERDINAND.*) My child is sick with love then, is she?

MIRANDA: Worse father. I have disobeyed you. I told him my name.

PROSPERO: I see. And does he love you?

MIRANDA: Above all heaven and earth. Beyond all limit of what there is in the world, he does love, prize and honour me.

PROSPERO: Truly?

MIRANDA: (*Spinning round.*) Oh, a thousand thousand!

PROSPERO: (*Beat.*) And what does that mean?

MIRANDA: I don't know, father, but he said it to me, and it sounded as if all my heart had leapt into his voice and

I called him husband. And he called me wife. And I
cried even though I was happy. And he placed his hand
in mine and…

PROSPERO: Go now, Miranda, return the log of wood
to the prisoner. And I promise to somewhat lighten his
load. (*Throws magic dust in the air.*)

MIRANDA: Yes, father. (*She picks up log.*) It's much lighter
now. Thank you. (*She runs off.*)

PROSPERO: (*Watches her go.*) I'll to my book
For yet ere supper-time must I perform
Much business appertaining. (*He exits.*)

*ARIEL enters and flies around the room. She rests on
the head of a child and then flies off again.*

ARIEL: (*Offstage.*) Thou liest!

STEPHANO enters carrying CALIBAN.

They are followed by TRINCULO.

STEPHANO: Trinculo, leave the monster alone. Call him
a liar again, and Stephano will remove a couple of your
teeth. No, I will.

TRINCULO: I said nothing. I swear on my life.

STEPHANO: Well, good. Shut up then. Again, monster.
Tell me about the island.

CALIBAN: (*Into STEPHANO's ear.*) You shall be lord over
all the island, for I know you can. But first I will take
you to where Prospero sleeps and there you may knock
a nail into his head.

ARIEL: (*Popping out, perhaps from TRINCULO's hat.*) Thou
liest! Thou canst not.

TRINCULO gets up.

STEPHANO: Trinculo, what did I just say? Shut up. Interrupt the monster one more time and I'll interrupt your face! Right!

TRINCULO: What did I do? I didn't do anything.

STEPHANO: You just called him a liar. (*Turns.*)

ARIEL: (*Appears once more from the hat.*) Thou liest!

TRINCULO gets up.

STEPHANO: So now I'm a liar, am I?

TRINCULO: What?

STEPHANO hits TRINCULO.

STEPHANO: Now shut up.

TRINCULO looks emotionally hurt and walks far away from them.

Come, monster, tell me about this Prospero again. But in that soft voice. The one that sounds like sweet rum on an autumn sunset.

CALIBAN: Why, as I told thee, tis a custom with him I'th'afternoon to sleep. There thou mayst brain him,

TRINCULO: (*To children.*) Brain him, la di da.

CALIBAN: Having first seized his books;

TRINCULO: Books, la di da. (*Beat as he thinks.*) I can read books.

CALIBAN: Or with a log batter his skull.

TRINCULO: Now, that's horrible.

CALIBAN: Or paunch him with a stake.

TRINCULO: Oooh, but I could kill a steak right now.

STEPHANO: Oh would you please shut up!

TRINCULO is quiet.

Now monster. Something about his books.

CALIBAN: Remember
First to possess his books, for without them
He's but a sot. Burn but his books.

STEPHANO nods.

CALIBAN: And that most deeply to consider, is
The beauty of his daughter.

STEPHANO: Is it so brave a lass?

CALIBAN: Ay, lord, she will become thy bed, I warrant,
And bring thee forth brave brood.

STEPHANO picks up CALIBAN and swings him around.

STEPHANO: Monster, I will kill this man for you. I'll marry his daughter and make her my queen and you and Trinculo can be my deputies. What do you think, Trink? What do you think of my plan?

TRINCULO: (*Beat.*) Excellent.

STEPHANO: Oh, Trink, I am sorry I hit you. No, I am. Now come here. Let's have a group hug.

They all hug.

Music.

What's that?

TRINCULO: It's music. But there's nobody playing it!

They hide behind the puppet, CALIBAN.

The music changes slightly as CALIBAN's speech starts. It is recorded and both actors manipulate the puppet.

CALIBAN: Be not afeared, the isle is full of noises,

Sounds, and sweet airs, that give delight and hurt not.
Sometimes a thousand twangling instruments
Will hum about mine ears; and sometime voices,
That if I then had waked after long sleep,
Will make me sleep again; and then in dreaming,
The clouds methought would open, and show riches
Ready to drop upon me, that when I waked
I cried to dream again.

TRINCULO: The sound is going away. Let's follow it.
(*Runs off.*)

STEPHANO: This will prove a brave kingdom to me,
where I shall have my music for nothing. Lead monster!

They exit.

*ARIEL enters as a human with puppet like features.
She runs around the room examining the children. She
examines her arms and her head. One of her arms is
spirit. The other is human. Something is different. She
is getting closer to freedom.*

PROSPERO: (*Entering.*) Yes, Ariel. Soon. But first, there is
more work.

ARIEL adorns a Harpy version of ARIEL.

For meanwhile, in another part of the island, our other
enemies are preparing to feast upon a banquet that I
have prepared for them. The King, Antonio, Sebastian.
Stand. (*Beat. To children.*) Come stand. Stand and eat. (*To
rest of audience.*) But as they lent forward to eat, the banquet of food vanished into the air and Ariel appeared
to them as a Harpy! (*PROSPERO has put on his cloak.*)
Magic spirit, do your worst!

*Music and lightning. Possible children make noise.
PROSPERO wields magic as if helping to manipulate
the Harpy.*

ARIEL: You are three men of sin, whom Destiny
　　　Has caused to belch up you. And on this island
　　　Being most unfit to live, I have made you mad.
　　　You Fools! You men of sin! If you could hurt
　　　Your swords are now too massy for your strengths,
　　　And will not be uplifted. But remember –
　　　For that's my business to you – that you three
　　　From Milan did supplant good Prospero.
　　　The powers, delaying, not forgetting, have
　　　Incensed the seas and shores, yea all the creatures
　　　Against your peace. Thee of thy son, great King
　　　They have bereft; and do pronounce by me
　　　Lingering perdition – worse than any death.
　　　Upon your heads is nothing but heart's sorrow!

Music changes as ARIEL runs off.

PROSPERO: Bravely the figure of this harpy hast thou
　　　Performed my Ariel; a grace it had devouring.
　　　And these, mine enemies are all knit up
　　　In their distractions. They now are in my power;
　　　And in these fits I leave them, while I visit
　　　Young Ferdinand, whom they suppose is drowned.
　　　(*Motions the three to sit.*)

Music fades.

End of Act Three.

ACT FOUR

FERDINAND enters.

PROSPERO holds his cloak in his hands.

PROSPERO: And now to my future son. Ferdinand, come forward. I know I have treated you harshly, but now, as you prepare to be my son, remember that her love should make amends for my harsh treatment.

FERDINAND: More than amends, father. If I may call you father. For she is what I am. She's what I do. All I live for now.

PROSPERO: Beautifully spoken. Therefore go in, and sit with her, talk to her. Prepare yourselves for your marriage day. You have worked enough.

FERDINAND: Thank you father. (*He exits.*)

PROSPERO: What, Ariel! My industrious servant Ariel!

ARIEL: (*Enters.*) What would my potent master? Here I am.

PROSPERO: Thou and thy meaner fellows your last

service
Did worthily perform; and I must use you
In such another trick. Go bring the rabble.
Incite them to quick motion, for I must
Bestow upon the eyes of this young couple
Some vanity of mine art.

ARIEL: Before you can say 'come' and 'go'
And breathe twice and cry 'so, so'.
(*Starts to go but stops.*)
Do you love me master? No?

PROSPERO: Dearly my delicate Ariel.

ARIEL rushes to kiss him but then runs round the audience and exits.

Music plays.

PROSPERO: Ye elves of hills, brooks, standing lakes, and

groves;
And ye that on the sands with printless foot
Do chase the ebbing Neptune, and do fly him
When he comes back; you demi-puppets, that
By moonshine do the green sour ringlets make,
Whereof the ewe not bites;

ARIEL enters, carrying a photograph of MIRANDA's face, or some representation of MIRANDA, lovingly in front of her. She dances around PROSPERO and exits.

And you, whose pastime
Is to make midnight mushrooms, by whose aid –
Weak masters though you are – I have bedimmed
The noontide sun, called forth the mutinous winds,
And twixt the green sea and the azured vault
Have I given fire, and by the spurs plucked up
The pine and cedar. Farewell.

ARIEL enters, carrying a photograph of FERDINAND's face, or some representation of FERDINAND, lovingly in front of her. She dances around PROSPERO and exits.

For this rough magic
I here abjure. And when I have required
Some heavenly music, I'll break my staff,
And deeper than did ever plummet sound
I'll drown my book. But first, Ariel, come!

ARIEL: (*Appearing.*) Thy thoughts I cleave to. What's thy

pleasure?

PROSPERO: Spirit,

We must prepare to meet with Caliban.
Say again, where didst thou leave these varlets?

ARIEL: I'th'filthy mantld pool beyond your cell
There dancing up to th'chins, that the foul lake
O'er – stunk their feet.

PROSPERO: This was well done, my bird!
Go bring them hither!

ARIEL: I go, I go. (*Exits.*)

PROSPERO: Caliban.
A devil, a born devil, on whose nature
Nurture can never stick. I will plague them all
Even to roaring.

PROSPERO uses magic to set a washing line of clothes.

TRINCULO enters as PROSPERO exits.

TRINCULO: (*Beat.*) I smell…of horse piss. I swear on
my life. I smell worse than that monster. We follow this
music, cos it's pretty, you know what I mean? And then
before I know it I'm knee deep in… Wait a minute.
Would you look at those clothes? Hey, Stephano, lord of
all the islands. I said King Stephano!

STEPHANO enters with CALIBAN.

STEPHANO: (*Entering.*) Of course I'll kill this Prospero,
monster. Just as soon as we… (*Sees clothes.*) Completely
rethink our wardrobe. (*Drops the puppet.*) Oh, sorry,
monster. No, I am.

TRINCULO: Look Stephano. They're blue!

STEPHANO: Blue is the new pink, Trink. Pass it here.

TRINCULO: All yours, my lord.

STEPHANO: Stop struggling monster. Trinculo, hold
the monster while I get changed. (*Throws puppet to*

37

TRINCULO: You hold him. This monster is starting to do my head in. (*Throws him back.*)

STEPHANO: Get off, will you monster! This is not a flipping frippery! (*Throws CALIBAN to TRINCULO.*) It's genuine silk!

TRINCULO: Yeah, shut up Monster! (*Throws him back.*) Do I look fat in this?

There is the sound of dogs.

What's that noise?

STEPHANO: Ouch. Something just bit me.

TRINCULO: Invisible dogs! What are we going to do? Ouch.

STEPHANO: I think there's only one thing to do.

TRINCULO: And what's that. Ouch!

STEPHANO: Runaway!

Music.

STEPHANO/TRINCULO: Runaway! Runaway!

They run around the audience being attacked by the invisible dogs, STEPHANO carrying CALIBAN.

STEPHANO: Help! Help! Ouch, that hurt. No, it did.

TRINCULO has run out, and reappeared as ARIEL.

She continues to run around.

Ouch!

Eventually they run into each other. They look at the audience. Then at each other.

ARIEL: Raaagh!

STEPHANO: Aaah! (*Running off.*) Runaway! Runaway! Runaway!

ARIEL laughs as STEPHANO and CALIBAN run off and she claps her hands. Then she is suddenly overcome by something. She holds her hands up and stares at them. She touches her face. PROSPERO is letting his power over her go and she can feel it inside her. She sings and dances.

ARIEL: Where the bee sucks, there suck I
    In a cowslip's bell I lie
    There I couch when owls do cry
    On the bat's back I do fly
    After summer merrily
    Merrily shall I live now
    Where the bee sucks, I'll live now
    Under blossoms that hang on the bough.

She curtsies.

PROSPERO enters and applauds her. He wears his cloak.

PROSPERO: Now does my project gather to a head
    My charms crack not, my spirits obey. Say,
    How fares the King and's followers?

ARIEL: (*Pointing to the three children.*) Confined together
    Just as you left them.
    They cannot budge till your release.
    Your charm so strongly works 'em
    That if you now beheld them, your affections
    Would become tender.

PROSPERO: Dost thou think so, spirit?

ARIEL: Mine would, sir, were I human.

PROSPERO: And mine shall.
    Go, release them Ariel.

My charms I'll break, their senses I'll restore,
And they shall be themselves.

ARIEL: I'll fetch them, sir.

PROSPERO places the ship on the table.

PROSPERO: And so it came to pass that I once more
was re-united with my family, my friends and my foes.
Behold, I am the rightful Duke of Milan, Prospero. And
so, I shake the hand of the King of Naples. Thank you
for looking after Milan, but I think I should like your
son to look after it now. Seeing as he has just married
my daughter. (*He takes the crown from the child and points
to ARIEL who enters with a large image of MIRANDA and
FERDINAND, together and in love.*) Look not so amazed.
Your son is safe and alive, sir. And he is married to
my Miranda. And the gods look down on them with
blessings. You shall be with them soon.

ARIEL exits.

My dear friend, Gonzalo. (*He embraces the teacher.*) See, I
was thrust out of Milan so that my daughter could, one
day, rule Naples. You are a sight for sore eyes, friend.
(*Beat. Stares at teacher a moment.*) Even though you look
so much older. You will soon see my daughter and she
will kneel and kiss your hand and be amazed!

ARIEL: (*Kneeling and speaking for MIRANDA.*) O wonder!
How beauteous mankind is! O brave new world
That has such people in't!

PROSPERO: 'Tis new to thee.

ARIEL: (*Standing again.*) Master, I feel so different.

PROSPERO: Soon, Ariel. Soon.

She exits.

Now, I do not expect you to say sorry, brother. I do not

expect you to say anything. Or you, Sebastian. But I forgive you, hideous though you both are. (*He takes hats or headdresses from them.*) You shall, however, return to me my precious Milan.

ARIEL: (*Returning with the puppet CALIBAN.*) And here's another, master, that would have your throne.

PROSPERO: Caliban, do you tremble now with fear? Shall you be bitten to death for this? No. I forgive you. And your foolish friends. But I think you'll choose your Gods more carefully in the future.

CALIBAN nods and kisses PROSPERO's feet. Music plays. As PROSPERO delivers his next speech, ARIEL places the puppets gently back into the ship, and CALI-BAN back into his cave. PROSPERO addresses the audience.

PROSPERO: You do look, my sons, in a moved sort
As if you were dismayed. Be cheerful, sirs,
Our revels now are ended; these our actors
Are melted into air, into thin air;
And like the baseless fabric of this vision
The cloud-capped towers, the gorgeous palaces,
The solemn temples, the great globe itself
Yea, all which it inherit, shall dissolve,
And like this insubstantial pageant faded
Leave not a rack behind. We are such stuff
As dreams are made on; and our little life
Is rounded with a sleep.

PROSPERO wraps his cloak around the tree. He pulls pieces of the chess board off the table and they fall to the floor. He throws the pages of the books into the air. As he does so ARIEL is struck within her very soul. She lifts her head up to the stars, becomes totally human, and she is free.

Ariel, I am vexed. (*PROSPERO starts to stoop.*)

Now my charms are all o'erthrown,
And what strength I have's mine own.

ARIEL: (*She goes to steady him.*) Which is most faint.

PROSPERO: (*To audience.*) Now 'tis true
I must be here confined by you
Or sent to Naples, let me not,
Since I have my dukedom got.

ARIEL: And pardoned the deceiver,

PROSPERO: Dwell
In this bare island, by your spell
But release me from my bands

ARIEL: With the help of your good hands.

PROSPERO: Gentle breath of yours my sails
Must fill, or else my project fails
Which was to please. Now I want

ARIEL: Spirits to enforce, art to enchant,
(*She gets him a walking stick.*)

PROSPERO: And my ending is despair,
Unless I be relieved by prayer

ARIEL: Which pierces so, that it assaults
Mercy itself, and frees all faults.

PROSPERO: As you from crimes would pardoned be.

ARIEL: Let your indulgence. (*A lump builds in her throat and she stops. She looks at PROSPERO.*) Goodbye my Lord.

PROSPERO: Goodbye Sweet Ariel. You are free.

ARIEL hugs him.

He kisses her gently on her forehead and lets go.

She runs to the other side of the audience.

He starts to exit.

PROSPERO: (*Turning.*) Now. Let your indulgence. Set *me* free.

PROSPERO is gone.

ARIEL runs after him. Then stops, and remembers. She looks at the puppet of PROSPERO that still lies at the back of the stage. She picks it up, like a treasured doll, and runs off the other side. The wind picks up and billows against the cloak on the tree. The pages blow around and the island is left as it was once found.

The End.

KING RAM AND THE TARTAN SNOW BABY

for performance to 7 year olds and older

with thanks to Robert Burns and the Brothers Grimm

Characters

SHADWELL
a Supersheep (Edgar)

DANIEL
a boy of ten

KING RAM
(King Lear)

CORDELIA
a young sheep (Cordelia)

REGAN
her older sister (Regan)

VICTORIA RED
a sorceress (Goneril)

EDDIE THE MONKEY
a chimpanzee (The Fool)

HAGGIS
a harpy (Edmund)

OLD RED RIDING HOOD
an old half fairy (Kent)

King Ram and the Tartan Snow Baby was first performed at The Sherman Theatre, Cardiff on 2 February 2002, with the following cast:

SHADWELL, Sharon James

DANIEL, Peter Walsh

KING RAM, Alastair Sill

CORDELIA, Natalie Morgan

REGAN, Ciaran O'Keefe

VICTORIA RED, Jane Gull

EDDIE THE MONKEY, Greg Ashton

HAGGIS, Richard Colvin/David Colvin

OLD RED RIDING HOOD, Trish Murphy

WOLF/RANDOM PENGUIN, Mark Thomas

WHITE FAIRY/BANANA, Anna Murphy

VOICE OF THE MIRROR, Rosy Greenwood

Directors, Greg Ashton and Tabitha Owens

Designer, James North

Musical Director, David Last and Gareth Ellis

Stage Manager, Eli Atkinson

Note

Although the script is based on *King Lear*, it also represents Part Four of *The Supersheep Chronicles*.

Prologue

Song: Supersheep.

ALL: (*Offstage.*) Supersheep (*x 8*)
    Are go!

SHADWELL, the Supersheep rushes in, singing.

SHADWELL: Supersheep
    Supersheep
    For truth
    For justice
    For the golden fleece
    Will fight for peace
    Forever and a day
    Bleat three times and pray
    For Supersheep!

    (*Speaks.*) And so, once more
    Begins the story of a sheep
    Deep in the mountains
    Deep in trouble,
    This King of Sheep
    This Ram of Old
    This Old King Ram.

    But first
    Worse than that
    The story of a fairy
    The heart of a fairy
    Pure and kind
    The White Fairy lost in the snow
    Knowing no one
    Running from the wolf pack
    Running from the black ambush of the wolves
    Saved…

    By a boy
    Saved by the boy with the huge hands

DANIEL appears in a spotlight, wearing boxing gloves.

Huge hands box those wolves and they flee
Weeeeeeeeee watch the wolves whimper away!

DANIEL: Stay there, fairy.

SHADWELL: Says the boy
The Boy with the huge hands

DANIEL: I'll help you
I'll carry you.

SHADWELL: But wait.
The boy's huge hands feel the huge belly.
Like jelly, it moves inside the white fairy.
Something is coming
A fairy something is coming in the snow.
Nowhere to go for shelter.
Nowhere to go in this helter-skelter wilderness.
Lost in the snow,
The brave boy and the beautiful fairy bring forth the
fairy child.
The mother weeps with joy
The boy weeps at the beauty of the scene.

But wait.
The fairy is weak.
Her crystal fades.
Fading fast as the snowflakes fall around her.
It is her time to go and find the place of peace.
And so the brave fairy.
Let us call her Gwen.
And so the brave fairy
Held by the brave boy
Carries the child's smile in her heart.
And her life floats away.
And she knows no more the cruelty of wolves.
Or Man.

But wait.
The boy
Let us call him Daniel
He digs deep into the earth
And buries the white fairy in a casket of lilies
And with the baby under his protection
He ventures onwards to find the fairy child's father.
Armed with nothing more than a pair of huge hands
And a bottle of milk…

SHADWELL exits.

DANIEL comes on, carrying the baby on his front. He has his boxing gloves in a little rucksack on his back. The baby is crying.

DANIEL: It's all right Snowy. We'll find your dad. Here. Have some of this. (*He feeds her some milk, and she stops crying.*) See, that's better. Isn't it?

KING RAM: (*Running on.*) Baaah! Baaah! Baaah! Baby! Baby! Nonononono! Don't let it grow up, baby boy. Don't let it grow up! Nonononono!

DANIEL: (*Running off, chased by KING RAM.*) Leave me alone.

Scene 1

France.

CORDELIA runs on and looks around.

CORDELIA: Shadwell! Shadwell! Oh where is she? What was it my mother taught me? Bleat three times and pray. Oh I hope she can hear me this time. (*She closes her eyes.*) Baaah! Baaah! Baaah! (*She looks around once more.*) Oh it's no use. I'll never find her. (*The sound of music.*)

SHADWELL: (*Running on.*) Supersheep to the rescue!

CORDELIA: Shadwell! Is it really you?

SHADWELL: Last time I looked in the mirror, love. But then that was over two days ago, so I don't know. You got a mirror?

CORDELIA: No.

SHADWELL: Then I guess you're going to have to take my word for it.

CORDELIA: Where are the other Supersheep?

SHADWELL: Fighting for truth and justice! Now, how can I help?

CORDELIA: Well, my father, King Ram…

SHADWELL: King Ram? He's one of my heroes, he is. Why didn't you say so? How is he? I heard that he is one of the wisest sheep in all…

CORDELIA: He's in serious danger.

SHADWELL: Danger? What from? Don't tell me, from a giant Octopus? From a flying Dragon? From a…

CORDELIA: From a sheep.

SHADWELL: (*Beat.*) Excuse me. Wait one second. Wait one blessed minute. Did you just say 'From a sheep'?

CORDELIA: Yes. From my sister, Regan.

SHADWELL: Your sister? Regan? No, it couldn't be? Are you sure it wasn't a wolf in sheep's clothing?

CORDELIA: Quite sure.

SHADWELL: Oh my lovelies, my precious, my sweets. This is a sad day. Sheep turning against sheep. Daughter turning against father. We are becoming a generation of savages. Worse than that, even. Where is your father now?

CORDELIA: I don't know, but Regan's left him out in the mountains, and it's snowing.

SHADWELL: But how did this all happen?

CORDELIA: Well, Daddy wanted Regan and I to look after the flock for him. So he decided to split the sixty-eight fields in two. We'd each look after half. But first he held this huge public meeting, with all the sheep councils present. We had to tell everyone how much we loved him.

SHADWELL: Why?

CORDELIA: I don't know why. All I remember is that Regan brought me this piece of paper.

Song: The Plan.

REGAN enters, carrying paper.

REGAN: Sister – dear
Here is what I've written out
Sister – love
This is what you'll say
Take your time
Finally our time has come
Sister – this
Will be taken from father
And ours by the end of the day

CORDELIA: I cannot say this
For this is not true
What do you mean by this?
What are you planning to do?

REGAN: Sister – think
This is what he's waiting for
Sister – now
This is what he wants
It's only – words
We won't get another chance

Old things die
So give father a show or
You'll throw our future away.

REGAN: (*Speaks.*) Here he comes.

KING RAM: Let's keep this short
Let's keep it simple
I'm splitting my land
In this grand design

I can roam free
I can live simple
For I can be safe in the knowledge
That each half is tended
By these splendid daughters of mine.

REGAN: (*Speaks.*) We understand, Father.

KING RAM: I want to be sure
For this is the test
Which of you favours me more?
Which of you loves me the best?
(*Speaks.*) Regan?

REGAN: Father, I love you more than life itself
Father, I love you more than grace or beauty
Rather, I have no friend in joy or wealth
Unless I can spend it showing you
How much my duty to you is my love!

KING RAM: (*Speaks.*) And now Cordelia. Let's see if you
can gain the bigger half. Thirty fields for your sister.
Thirty-eight for you.

REGAN: (*Speaks.*) Go on, sister.

CORDELIA: Father, I… Father, I…

KING RAM: (*Speaks.*) Father, I… Father I… Father I what?

CORDELIA: Baaah!

(*Music stops.*)

KING RAM: Baaah? What is this Baaah? Baaah is likely to see you stripped Baaare of everything I was going to give you.

CORDELIA: Father, my tongue can't say anything unless my heart feels it. And if my heart feels it, then I shouldn't need to say it. Not here, in front of all these sheep.

KING RAM: So you can't tell me you love me?

CORDELIA: Love shouldn't be a competition, Father.

KING RAM: Because you don't love me.

CORDELIA: That's not what I said, father.

KING RAM: But it's what you meant. You are no sheep of mine. Go. Leave this place. Go on, get out! Bleat for your supper! Regan, you can look after my whole kingdom, for you truly love me.

REGAN: Yes, Father, I do.

CORDELIA: But, Father.

KING RAM: (*Sings.*) Let's keep this short
    Let's keep it simple
    I wish to split
    Myself from you

REGAN: So just get out!
    He will not see you.

BOTH: You can be sure in the knowledge

KING RAM: That you are no daughter

REGAN: That you are no sister

KING RAM/REGAN: Yes, you are no daughter (sister) of Mine!

KING RAM exits.

REGAN: (*Looking at CORDELIA.*) Goodbye Cordelia.

CORDELIA: Look after him, Regan.

REGAN: I'll make sure he gets what he deserves. (*She exits.*)

SHADWELL starts crying.

CORDELIA: And then she turned all the other sheep against him, and made him go crazy. Are you all right?

SHADWELL: Oh, I'm sorry, I'm just a bit emotional, that's all. We'll save your father, even if he is doolally twist. Now, come on, follow me! Supersheep to the rescue!!

They run off.

SHADWELL and CORDELIA run back on.

SHADWELL: Sorry, love, I got a bit lost there. But I'm pretty sure it's this way! Supersheep to the rescue!!

They run off.

DANIEL, carrying the baby, runs on being chased by KING RAM.

DANIEL: Leave me alone!

They run off.

Scene 2

The Land of Colours.

Music.

VICTORIA RED enters.

VICTORIA: Ding Dong, the Fairy's Dead!
   How convenient for me.

I want her husband. She dies. And I didn't even lift a
finger.

Shame!
(*Flirting with the musician.*)
Oh, I do so love being bad
It's so much more tempting than being good?
(*Handing him her drink.*)
Don't you think?

He stops playing to take the drink.

For instance, that drink.
Is it full of intoxicating pleasure?
Or measured with two parts poison
To each part nice.
Sip it, taste it, try a little spice in your life.

The musician puts the drink down.

VICTORIA RED laughs a little.

Coward.
Musician, play me something rich with dread.

He plays.

For the White Fairy is dead.
And the Man of Colours, he grieves, he weeps, he
sleeps
in a lonely bed.
But soon
When the moon is lost
And his head is tossed in the sea of change
Then comes the frost of times forgotten
I'll make him forget the life he led
The wife who's dead
The tears he shed.
And soon he'll belong to Victoria Red.

VOICE: (*Off.*) Lady Victoria, please welcome Queen
Regan, the leader of the sheep in the sixty-eight fields.

VICTORIA: Oh, how depressing. I hate Sheep!

REGAN: Lady Victoria, I believe.

VICTORIA: Queen Regan.

REGAN: So this is the Land of Colours. I always wanted to see it for myself.

VICTORIA: I'm sorry everyone is so sad. But we are in mourning for the White Fairy. She disappeared six weeks ago, and now she's assumed to be dead.

REGAN: But you're wearing red. Aren't you supposed to wear black if someone dies?

VICTORIA: It's a deeper shade than my usual. Now. What do you want?

REGAN: I need your help.

VICTORIA: Oh, really? How nice, but I'm very busy.

REGAN: Yes, I'm sure. But my father, the old King Ram, has gone mad.

VICTORIA: Crazy?

REGAN: Absolutely bonkers!

VICTORIA: And you want me to help him?

REGAN: No, darling, I made him go crazy in the first place. But now my sister, Cordelia, is trying to save him.

VICTORIA: So, so what? What do I care? You may be Queen of the Sheep, but you're still just a sheep. And I hate sheep.

REGAN: But I know something you hate more than sheep.

VICTORIA: Bananas?

REGAN: No. Supersheep.

VICTORIA: What do you know of Supersheep?

REGAN: I know they've foiled your plans before. I know that you've tried to kill them all before.

VICTORIA: And I would have, if that interfering chicken hadn't warned one of them.

REGAN: Well, Cordelia has gone to get help from none other than Shadwell, the leader of the Supersheep.

VICTORIA: Tell me more.

REGAN: The Supersheep are in France, fighting for truth and justice. But Cordelia hopes to bring Shadwell here to lead an army and destroy me.

VICTORIA: Shadwell is coming here, on her own?

REGAN: Yes.

VICTORIA: Perfect.

REGAN: So you'll help me?

VICTORIA: I don't need to worry about you. I can just get rid of Shadwell, myself. That's all I care about.

REGAN: Oh, I think you'll help me.

VICTORIA: Give me one good reason why.

REGAN: Because I've brought you a gift. A chicken.

Beat.

VICTORIA: *The* chicken?

REGAN: Yes, the one that warned Shadwell. We found him, hiding in Gloucester.

VICTORIA: Where is he now?

REGAN: With my bodyguards.

VICTORIA: Well, then…hang him instantly.

REGAN: No. Pluck out his feathers.

VICTORIA: I like your style. Yes. Pluck out his feathers. Slowly. And then hang him. Now, where is this sister of yours?

REGAN: (*Giving her a piece of tartan.*) This is hers. It still has her scent.

VICTORIA: And where is your father?

REGAN: He was last seen in the mountains of Scotland, chasing a little boy and a baby.

VICTORIA: How ridiculous. A baby, you say?

REGAN: Yes, a baby wrapped in a tartan blanket.

VICTORIA stops.

VICTORIA: What? Tartan? What colour was the tartan?

REGAN: Green and red, with a golden hem. That's what my spies told me.

VICTORIA: (*Shaking REGAN.*) But that's the daughter of the White Fairy. That's the daughter of the Man of Colours. That's the only thing that stands between me and my future happiness!

REGAN: So the baby in the snow belongs to the Man of Colours?

VICTORIA: Yes. Another little inconvenience.

REGAN: I see.

VICTORIA: So, I'll make sure that your sister is stopped. But in return, I want you to do something for me.

REGAN: Anything.

VICTORIA: Kill the baby.

REGAN: Well, if I can I find it, of course.

VICTORIA: You'd better find it. Now get out! And don't forget, you're still a sheep.

REGAN leaves.

So, the baby's still alive. And on a mountain.

We hear the screams of a tortured chicken.

Well, then, its time I went on a little treasure hunt. But first to stir up the weather a little. Music.
Come storm of spider
Come blizzard of crow
Pour your fear on the mountains
For they near your insatiable blow! (*Runs off laughing.*)

CORDELIA and SHADWELL run across the stage.

SHADWELL: Supersheep to the rescue!

Scene 3

Scottish Mountains.

DANIEL runs on.

DANIEL: I think we lost him, Snowy.

KING RAM: (*Running on.*) Who you hiding from, baby boy?

DANIEL: Oh no! Look, I'm not a baby boy. I'm Daniel, and this is a baby.

KING RAM: Yes, well, little lambs grow up into big fat evil sheep. Take everything you got and leave you in a spot, an evil plot to see you weep. Baaah!

DANIEL: This isn't a lamb.

KING RAM: Same thing. Grows up into an evil thing, does a lamb.

DANIEL: Are you mad?

KING RAM: (*Beat.*) Mmm? Yes. Mad and bad, and thoroughly glad to make your acquaintance.

He offers his hand.

DANIEL goes to shake it and the KING pulls his hand away.

Baaah!

DANIEL: Please leave me alone.

KING RAM: I'll leave you alone if you'll answer a simple question.

DANIEL: Fine.

KING RAM: Is a blue fish a fish that is coloured blue, or a blue colour moulded into the shape of a fish?

DANIEL: I don't know what you are talking about. I'm not a fish.

KING RAM: This is going to be difficult, I see. (*Pointing at the audience.*) Sheep or children?

DANIEL: What?

KING RAM: Them there those thinking things in the clothes. Sheep or children?

DANIEL: Well, some children and some adults.

KING RAM: (*To the audience.*) Baaah! Repeat after me. Baaah! Come on, all of you. Baaah! Baaah! See, now, are they sheep or children? Ah, yes, there comes the paradox of Polly Anna Polly Clogs?

DANIEL: I don't understand.

KING RAM: It's all about how you see the world. That's what you learn from Polly Anna Polly Clogs. Now, take this baby.

DANIEL: She's called Baby Snow.

KING RAM: Boy or girl?

DANIEL: (*Beat.*) *She's* called Baby Snow.

KING RAM: Girl. Mmm, you've got a baby daughter.

DANIEL: Oh, she's not mine.

KING RAM: But if I put lots of white petals around her head, you have a baby sun…flower!

DANIEL: She's not a sunflower and she's not mine!

KING RAM: Sun Flower! Flower Power! Sun Flower! Flower Power!

DANIEL: I'm sorry about this Baby.

Enter EDDIE.

EDDIE: Hoo-hoo-hoo-hoo-Ha-ha-aaah-aaah!

DANIEL: What is going on, now? Who, in the name of Ben Nevis, are you?

The monkey stops and contemplates them both.

KING RAM: Look out, boy, it may be a trap.

DANIEL: It's a monkey.

KING RAM: A monkey?

EDDIE: Monkey? Hoo hoo-hoo-hoo-Ha-ha-aaah-aaah!

KING RAM: Are you sure it's not a sheep?

DANIEL: A sheep?

KING RAM: If you squint, perhaps?

DANIEL: It's a monkey!

KING RAM: A monkey?

EDDIE: Monkey? Hoo-hoo-hoo-hoo-Ha-ha-aaah-aaah!

KING RAM: It is indeed something rare and different! But beautiful, nonetheless.

DANIEL: It's going to snow again soon. We've got to find shelter.

KING RAM: No, no, let it snow. Fall, snow. We'll just see it all like Polly Anna.

DANIEL: Who?

KING RAM: If you see life like Polly Anna Polly Clogs, then nothing can ever harm you. Haven't you ever heard of Polly Anna?

EDDIE: It's a baby. A baby! Baby, baby, baby, hoo-hoo-hoo-hoo.

Song: Life in the 'I Don't Know'.

KING RAM: You can live life like the Polly Clogs
　　No, no, yes you can
　　See only flowers in the dirt
　　Like Polly Anna can
　　Polly ignores what seems logical
　　So Polly logically
　　Cleverly never gets hurt

DANIEL: (*Speaks.*) But who is she?

KING RAM: Polly lives in the Polly Clog world
　　Singing I see the pony that's only a cat
　　As a matter of fact I would rather forget
　　I'm a father.

DANIEL: (*Speaks.*) What?

KING RAM: Oh, yes, dear boy,
　　I can see the blue fish

I have known things that are true
You don't need answers if none of the questions make

sense
True?

DANIEL: (*Speaks.*) I'm a little confused here.

KING RAM: Is this a field or a fingernail? – I couldn't say
    Is this a girl or a goat? – I don't know
    Is this a boy or a bana-na-na?

EDDIE: Ba-na-na-na-na-na-na.

KING RAM: Is she a banana bowl-er hat? And
    That is the way we must look at the world
    In the I don't know what I'm talking ab-
    Out of my mouth are sprouting the words flying south
    Like a bird. Fly away.

EDDIE: Ooh ooh ooh.

KING RAM: When you see the blue fish
    You can wish you were a ewe
    You-oo-oo-oo see the charming
    For what it is n-n-n-n-n-n-not.

EDDIE: Ooh ooh ooh.

KING RAM: Ewe must show ewe some humanity
    So choose carefully your insanity
    Don't give in to your own vanity
    Just show that you simply don't know
    Live the life that you simply don't know
    What is life?
    I simply don't know.

DANIEL: That's all very interesting, but I'm trying to find
    this baby's father. And we need to find shelter –

Thunder and lightning.

– before the storm hits! Listen to the thunder!

KING RAM: Oh blow winds, crack your thunder cracks! Nothing can harm me more than an evil ewe!

DANIEL: A ewe?

KING RAM: A you-know-what. My daughters!

DANIEL: We need to find shelter, and soon!

EDDIE: Red! Hoo Hoo! Red!!!

DANIEL: Red?

KING RAM: No, blue. The blue fish is blue. See, boy, never trust a sheep.

DANIEL: It's not a sheep it's a monkey.

EDDIE: Monkey! (*EDDIE motions them to follow.*) Ooh, ooh, ooh, ahahaha!

DANIEL: Baby, how can you sleep through all this? All right, I'm coming. Come on Ram.

KING RAM: (*Drifts into lucidity.*) King Ram, dear boy.

DANIEL: King Ram, then, come on.

KING RAM: Do you think a sheep can disguise itself as a monkey?

DANIEL: Come on!

They all run off.

Scene 4

The Land of Colours.

VICTORIA: (*Entering.*) Well, treasure hunt over. (*Showing the musician the items.*) The middle finger of a naughty boy. The broken string of a rusty harp. And a haggis baked in cyanide. Good. Now don't tell anyone about this, and I may even give you some candy. You'd like that, wouldn't you? I thought you would. Now:
Come seas of the web
Come stream of the spider
Take these trinkets of dread
To sink deep inside her
And bring me a harpy tonight!

She throws them out of her window. There is a splash and smoke and the sound of bagpipes.

Then HAGGIS the Harpy appears.

HAGGIS: I am Haggis the Harpy. What is your bidding, mistress?

VICTORIA: Find me Shadwell the Supersheep. Use this. Follow the scent and it will lead you to Cordelia Sheep, and she'll lead you to Shadwell.

He sniffs the material.

HAGGIS: Your wish is my command.

He runs off.

VICTORIA: We'll meet again, Shadwell, but this time, my power is at its greatest. (*Turns to the musician.*) I've got work to do. The candy will have to wait!

She exits.

SHADWELL: (*Running across the stage, followed by CORD-ELIA.*) Can you hear bagpipes yet?

Exeunt.

Scene 5

Old Red Riding Hood's cottage.

RED enters, followed by the sheep, the boy, the baby and the monkey.

RED: So you boxed these wolves, helped bring the baby into the world, and then found this sheep in the mountains? Well, kid, you did the right thing coming here.

DANIEL: My name's Daniel.

RED: Pleased to meet you Daniel, my name is Old Red Riding Hood, but you can call me Red.

DANIEL: Old Red Riding Hood? What, like Little Red Riding Hood.

RED: Yes, that's right, kid, only older. I too have had the odd run in with a wolf. But I got swallowed up and I had to be saved by my father and a rather remarkable sheep.

DANIEL: A sheep.

KING RAM: I'm a sheep. Baaah!

RED: A Supersheep.

DANIEL: Wow.

RED: Of course now, I'd probably just box the wolf's nose, like you did.

DANIEL: Can you box, too?

RED: Well I used to kick box, but the bones break too easily now, so I had to give it up. Eddie, give the sheep something to eat.

EDDIE: Ooooh, ooooh, oooh, oooh…banana?

RED: Yes, all right.

EDDIE leads KING RAM to a corner.

DANIEL: How do you know that monkey?

RED: That's Eddie. I think he's actually a chimpanzee, but I can't be sure. I don't meet a great range. He was a birthday present from a couple of hedgehogs.

DANIEL: Oh, this just gets weirder and weirder.

RED: Now, kid, give the baby to me.

DANIEL: (*Handing the baby over.*) All right, if you promise to treat her gently.

RED: I will. (*Takes the baby.*) Wait one second. This child is half fairy. Like me.

DANIEL: I thought she was all fairy.

RED: No, if she was all fairy, she'd have wings.

DANIEL: But her mother was a fairy.

RED: I can see that. So was mine. But like me, her father was a human. Either way she is a very special baby.

DANIEL: Really?

RED: Oh, yes, there aren't many fairies around any more, Daniel. There's a woman who hates fairies so much, she has been slowly getting rid of us one by one.

DANIEL: What?

RED: Oh yes, she tried to kill me once, but my life crystal is lying safe, where she'll never find it. (*She draws him into her.*) Fifty thousand leagues under the sea. Right at the bottom of the ocean.

DANIEL: Wow. But why does she hate fairies so much?

RED: Because she loved the Man of Colours, and he married a fairy.

DANIEL: But fairies are beautiful. The one I met was the

most beautiful thing I'd ever seen.

RED: Well, fairies are renowned for their beauty, yes.

DANIEL: She was all in white, and around her was this ray of light. That reflected on the snow and made it sparkle.

RED: (*Getting up.*) Oh no. Look kid, we are all in grave danger.

DANIEL: What do you mean?

RED: Eddie, leave the sheep alone.

EDDIE: Ooh – Ooh?

RED: I need you to take this boy to France.

EDDIE: Ooh-ooh-ooh.

DANIEL: I don't want to go to France. I want to find Baby Snow's father. I don't even know who he is yet.

RED: Don't you see, kid, the Man of Colours is this baby's father. Her mother was the white fairy. And so that woman I talked about will want her dead.

DANIEL: What woman?

RED: Victoria Red.

DANIEL: Who?

KING RAM: Blue!

They all turn to look at him.

It's a blue fish.

RED: Yes, that'll do, sheep. That'll do. Now, Victoria Red mustn't find this baby before we find the Man of Colours.

DANIEL: But why go to France?

RED: Because the Supersheep are there. You'll have to get

to France, and once you're on French soil, bleat three times, and they'll come and help you.

DANIEL: What about Baby Snow?

RED: I'll look after her until you find Shadwell. Now go!

EDDIE: Hoo-hoo-hoo-hoo-Ha-ha-aaah-aaah!

DANIEL: Goodbye Baby Snow. Look after her.

RED: I will.

EDDIE leads DANIEL off.

Now, Baby Snow, look at all the fuss you've caused.

KING RAM: Baaah. Snow. Baaah. White Snow Baby. Snow White.

RED: Snow White. What a perfect name for you. Well, Snow White, I knew your mother and your grandmother, and her mother, too. And you are a very precious little individual.

The baby starts to cry.

No, no, no need to cry. Just sleep now.

Song: Lullaby.

Hush a little lullaby
It's time now to go to sleep
Hush a little memory
Of mother and child
Whenever you are all alone
You know she'll be there for you
Hush a little lullaby
And dream of her smile

Somewhere she's out there
Gazing at you
Somehow she knows

Your dreams will come true.

RED/KING RAM: Lalalalalala
Lalalaaalala

They repeat tune to 'la' as they exit.

Scene 6

The Land of Colours.

VICTORIA RED enters, followed by HAGGIS, who carries a map.

VICTORIA: So, Shadwell is already on her way to Scotland. Good work, Haggis.

HAGGIS: I aim to please, oh evil one.

VICTORIA: Now, I think we can lure them into a trap. Just about there, where the road leads into a gorge between the mountains.

HAGGIS: And then?

VICTORIA: And then we stir up a little avalanche.

HAGGIS: What about Regan sheep, your Victoriousness?

VICTORIA: Yes. Regan. (*Walks over to the musician.*) Hey, you, got any other instruments back there I could use?

He hands her a flute in a case.

She looks inside.

A flute. Perfect. (*To HAGGIS.*) I want you to give this to her and tell her to play it when the baby is dead. But first, to lace it with poison. So that when Regan plays the flute, she will die. Baaah! (*Laughs.*)

HAGGIS: You are inhuman. I dream of this kind of evil, but you live it.

VICTORIA: Come on, let's go and make some music.

They exit.

SHADWELL and CORDELIA run on.

CORDELIA: Are you sure you know where you are going?

SHADWELL: Who cares, this is fun!

They exit.

Scene 7

The Land of the Sheep.

REGAN enters, carrying the flute, followed by HAGGIS.

REGAN: So, I'm only to play the flute after the baby is dead, yes? Oh how simple. And in the mean time you'll destroy Shadwell and my sister.

HAGGIS: Absolutely. But you must remember to play the flute.

REGAN: Well then, I think I know where the child is. She's being hidden in Old Red Riding Hood's cabin. So, what are you waiting for?

HAGGIS runs off.

And when Shadwell is dead, I'm coming after you Victoria Red. (*She runs off.*)

Scene 8

The Mountains of Scotland.

EDDIE enters, followed by DANIEL.

DANIEL: Eddie, wait up. Are you sure you know where

you're going?

EDDIE: Hoo-hoo-hoo-hoo-Ha-ha-aaah-aaah! Where am I going?

DANIEL: To France.

EDDIE: Mais Oui! Mais Ooo! Hoo-hoo-hoo-hoo-Ha-ha-aaah-aaah!

DANIEL: Oh, this is useless. We've been walking for hours and all we seem to come near is mountains.

EDDIE: Ooh?

DANIEL: Let's face it; we're never going to find the Supersheep! Are we?

EDDIE: Hoo-hoo-hoo-hoo-Ha-ha-aaah-aaah!

DANIEL: I'm sorry, Eddie, I haven't a clue what you're talking about.

EDDIE: Baaah! Ooh ooh. Baaah! Oooh. Baaah!

DANIEL: Nice try, Eddie, but we're in Scotland. And the Supersheep are in France. They'll never hear us here. We're in the middle of nowhere.

SHADWELL: (*Rushing on, followed by CORDELIA.*) Supersheep to the rescue!

EDDIE: Ooh, ooh, ooh!

DANIEL: Maybe we are in France, after all.

CORDELIA: Shadwell, we haven't got time for this. We've got to get to my army, and save my father.

SHADWELL: I never ignore a genuine call for help. That's why they call me Shadwell the Genuine.

EDDIE: Ooh?

CORDELIA: They don't call you that.

SHADWELL: No, but don't you think it's got a fabulous ring to it.

DANIEL: Are you really Shadwell, the Supersheep!

SHADWELL: That's right, Cariad. The first. The finest.

CORDELIA: The fruitcake.

SHADWELL: Look love, it's your dad whose doolally twist, not me.

DANIEL: I need your help.

CORDELIA: Look, boy –

DANIEL: It's Daniel.

CORDELIA: I don't care. My father has been thrown out of his home by his own daughter.

Beat.

DANIEL: You?

CORDELIA: Well, yes of course she's a ewe; a ewe is a female sheep. Queen Regan?

DANIEL: Wait a minute, is your father King Ram?

SHADWELL: What do you know about King Ram?

DANIEL: We found him alone in a storm, so we took him to find shelter. (*To SHADWELL.*) He's bonkers.

CORDELIA: Where is he now?

DANIEL. With an old lady called Red.

SHADWELL: Old Red Riding Hood?

DANIEL nods.

Then he's in good hands, Cordelia. Red is one of my oldest friends.

RED: (*Voice off.*) And she is always with you.

SHADWELL: Yeah. Just here. Here in my heart.

DANIEL: Well, anyway, we need you to help protect us when we take Baby Snow to the Man of Colours.

EDDIE: Ooh ooh ooh.

CORDELIA: Protect you from what?

SHADWELL: From Victoria Red. Nasty piece of work: really evil.

EDDIE: Ooh, ooh.

SHADWELL: Nice hair, mind.

CORDELIA: Have you got a plan, Shadwell?

SHADWELL: Always.

DANIEL: So what is it?

SHADWELL: Um, give me a minute; it'll come to me.

EDDIE: Baah!

SHADWELL: That's it. We get to Red's place. Re-unite Cordelia with her father. Take this baby to the Land of Colours. Defeat Victoria Red. Give the Man of Colours the baby. Then fight Regan sheep's army and help King Ram regain the sixty-eight fields that belong to him.

DANIEL: And how do we do all that?

SHADWELL: I have no flaming idea.

CORDELIA: Well maybe we should get to Red's place first, and then decide.

EDDIE: Oooh, ooh, ohh, Haaah! Haah!

SHADWELL: What's wrong with the monkey?

DANIEL: Look!

HAGGIS the Harpy enters.

SHADWELL: Oh dear.

CORDELIA: What is it?

SHADWELL: It's a haggis harpy, one of the most danger-ous creatures in all Scotland!

EDDIE: Ooh, ooh, ooh, Haaah! Haah!

CORDELIA: What are we going to do?

HAGGIS: I think dying would be an appropriate manoeu-vre, little sheep.

SHADWELL: Oh dear, there's only one-way to defeat a harpy when it's trying to kill you.

DANIEL: How?

HAGGIS: Yes, how exactly do you do that? I'm dying to know.

SHADWELL: Text book stuff, Haggis. (*To CORDELIA.*) The oldest trick in the book.

CORDELIA: Which is?

SHADWELL: (*Beat.*) Runaway! Runaway!

They all run out chased by HAGGIS.

Scene 9

Old Red Riding Hood's Cabin.

REGAN creeps in. The baby is in a cot. KING RAM sleeps in the rocking chair.

REGAN: So, this is Old Red Riding Hood's place. And there's my father, the mad old fool. Hello daddy dear-est. What's it like in the land of cuckoo? What's wrong, Cat got your tongue?

KING RAM: Visions, away! I know you've come to haunt me! But I have Polly Anna Polly Clogs. So I don't know you. Be gone!

REGAN: Sorry, you old relic, Polly's wrong this time. I'm very real! (*Sings.*) Father, I love you more than life itself. (*She rocks the chair until he falls on the floor.*) There. Feel better now.

KING RAM: Baah! You're not real. I've never seen you. Never!

REGAN: But I'm here.

KING RAM: Never. Never. Never. Never. Never.

REGAN: (*Prodding him.*) Regan. Regan. Regan. Regan. Real! And look, Daddy, look at this flute. Remember how you loved the flute being played to you. Well soon I'm going to play the flute for you again: only after I kill this wee baby.

KING RAM: She told me what I wanted to hear. She told me I was a white sheep, baaah, even though I was a black one.

REGAN: What are you muttering about, you old fossil. Of course you're a white sheep. Now, watch this. Hello, little baby. Time to say goodnight. (*She looks around and sees a stone. She picks it up and goes to kill the baby.*)

KING RAM: Noooo! (*He rushes forward and grabs her hand.*) Help! Baaah! Baaaah!

REGAN: Get off me you senile old goat! (*She pushes him to the floor.*)

KING RAM: Baaah! Baaaah!

RED rushes in.

RED: What's going on? Stop that. (*Beat.*) Get away from

her, you witch!

REGAN: No.

RED uses her power to stop her and forces her to drop the stone.

RED: I may be old, but I'm still half fairy, and I haven't tasted a lamb casserole in a long time. So get out, before I send for the Supersheep!

REGAN: Ha! The Supersheep? Right now, Victoria Red is destroying their leader. She's setting a trap for them. And even you're not powerful enough to stop her!

RED: I said get out!

REGAN: Fine! But I need my flute.

RED: Out!

RED lunges and REGAN runs off.

The flute is left.

KING RAM picks it up.

KING RAM: (*Shaking his head.*) Never leave the baby alone.

RED: I know, sheep. I also knew that you'd protect her. No matter how your mind has been damaged, you still know right from wrong.

KING RAM: Blue fish?

RED: King Ram, I need you to take this baby downstairs and lock yourself in. Here is the key. I have the other. No one can get in without it. You'll both be safe there.

KING RAM: Flute?

RED: Yes, you can take the flute. And there's plenty of milk for the baby. But I have to go and save Shadwell and the others. Before it's too late.

KING RAM: Baaah!

RED: Yes, good luck to the both of us!

They run in opposite directions.

Scene 10

The Scottish Mountains.

VICTORIA RED enters followed by HAGGIS.

VICTORIA: Right, Haggis, I need you to lead them to this spot, between these two mountains.

HAGGIS: And then?

VICTORIA: And then… The avalanche, my sweet soft sheep guts. But first, we'll need to shift the snow a little. Music.

The musician plays.

Come shift the snow from its seat
Come sleet and ice from your bed
Come hold till the victims advance
Come dance with the power of Victoria Red.

She dances while HAGGIS sings.

Song: The Avalanche Dance.

HAGGIS: Now let the hour of hate come upon you
Dance with the power of Amazon
Here let the evil state be revealed
Believe in the feet of babylon
Anger will guide you in the dance
Vengeance provide the sound

Nature will weep

For deep in the ground
The thundering echoes flow!

There!
Soon!
Beware!
Be still!
The mountains dance
Destroying all we know
A spider spins a death within the snow.

Now see the moon dance, hiding the sun
For one who will soon be glorious
Now see the flame dance night out of day
Make way for the name victorious

Anger enfold her in the dance
Vengeance will hold her still
Dance for the dead
See white turning red
Tonight all the gates of hell will open

Now!
See!
And bleat all you can for the golden fleece
Your fight for peace
Your woolly wonderwall
Bleat three times but no one hears the call.

VICTORIA: I'll kill them all.

BOTH: Avalanche
    Prepare to
    Kill them all.

VICTORIA: (*Speaks.*) Now, after them!

He runs off and she dances out.

OLD RED appears.

RED: Baah! Baaah! Baaah! Oh Shadwell, I hope you're

still alive!

She runs off, as SHADWELL, EDDIE, DANIEL and CORDELIA run on being chased by HAGGIS.

SHADWELL: I can hear Red calling me!

CORDELIA: I think that's the least of our worries!

EDDIE: Oooh Ooh, aaah, aaah!

DANIEL: Runaway! Runaway!

They run off.

OLD RED runs on being pursued by HAGGIS.

RED: Shadwell! Shadwell!

REGAN runs on being chased by VICTORIA RED, who carries an axe.

REGAN: I did my best!

VICTORIA: Well, do better next time, and don't forget to play that flute!

A chase ensues. At some point the group, EDDIE at the back, are being chased by a giant banana. EDDIE turns and sees the banana.

EDDIE: Banana!

He chases the banana off, but returns being pursued by the HAGGIS. The running around continues until SHADWELL, EDDIE, DANIEL and CORDELIA end up on the stage alone.

SHADWELL: I think we've escaped them, boys bach. I think we're safe.

CORDELIA: But where are we?

EDDIE: Ooh?

DANIEL: We appear to be below a rather large amount of snow.

VICTORIA: (*Entering.*) Yes. That would appear so!

SHADWELL: It's a trap!

CORDELIA: Let's get out of here!

HAGGIS appears in the smoke playing bagpipes.

VICTORIA: Too late!!!!!

ALL: Avalanche!!!!!

There is an avalanche and a huge sheet of snow covers the four of them.

VICTORIA: And goodbye to baaaaaaaaaaaad rubbish! Come on, Haggis; let's see whether that Sheep has killed the baby yet.

HAGGIS: What about the hooded Red one?

VICTORIA: She's old. Old people get weak. Old people die. She's not strong enough to face me. And without Shadwell, the Supersheep are useless. Just to get rid of the baby, and then I win. (*Stops for a second.*) Winning is everything. Always remember that. Everything!

HAGGIS: Whatever you say, mistress. Whatever you say!

They exit, laughing.

OLD RED enters, careful that they don't see her.

RED: Oh, no. Oh no. Shadwell. Where are you? Can you hear me under all that snow? Can you hear me?

Song: Here in my Heart.

Here in my heart
There is a bond
(*Speaks.*) Shadwell!

You are here for me
I am here forever your friend
(*Speaks.*) Oh, where are you, Shadwell?
There to the end
(*Speaks.*) It's Red.
We will never part
You are always here in my heart

SHADWELL: We're down here! Underneath the snow!

RED: Where?

SHADWELL: Here.

RED: Are you all still alive?

SHADWELL: Yes, we're in an air pocket, but we're running out of air. The boy is already passing out.

EDDIE: Oooh, ooh!

RED: Right, I'm going to have to raise the sun.

SHADWELL: Quickly.

RED: Okay, I'm going to need some help. We need to raise the sun in order to melt the snow. Now, can I have some helpers? Come on sir, we need some big helpers too. We can raise the sun if we all work together. (*Taking a parachute with the sun drawn on it and spreading it over the snow.*) Now, everyone take an edge and when I say, I want you all to lift the sun up into the air as high as it will go. But you've got to hold on really tight. Okay. Ready. One two three, lift!

They lift the parachute so that it floats above the snow sheet.

That was good but we can do better. On my count. One two three! And again. One, two, three!

The sheet starts to be pulled away.

It's melting. One more time. All count with me this time. One, two, three!

The sheet is pulled away and DANIEL coughs as he takes in air.

EDDIE examines the audience.

SHADWELL stands up.

SHADWELL: You did it, Red. You did it! You raised the sun!

RED: With a little help from my friends. You can all sit down, now. And thank you.

SHADWELL: But when did Victoria Red grow so powerful.

DANIEL: How are we going to stop her?

RED: I think I have an idea. But first, we need to get back to the baby and King Ram.

CORDELIA: How is he?

RED stares at her.

I'm Cordelia, his daughter.

RED: In which case, take this key, and look after him. Shadwell, you join Cordelia's army and destroy the army of Regan sheep. And then you and the kid go back to my cabin and wait for me there. Eddie, you come with me.

EDDIE: Ooh? Ooh, ooh.

DANIEL: Where are you going?

RED: To find a mirror. It once belonged to Helen of Troy.

SHADWELL: Helen of Troy? The face that launched a thousand sheeps?

RED: Almost. Now hurry.

They run off. EDDIE starts to head off, too.

Eddie, wait. I'm weak, Eddie, I'm not so young any more.

EDDIE goes and helps her offstage.

But you mustn't let the others know.

EDDIE: Ooh? Ooh, ooh, ooh.

RED: Oh, Eddie, I don't mind getting old. I've had a wonderful life. I've had adventures people only dream of, I've been up into the clouds; I've even been into the future. But I won't be here forever, and this mirror may be the only thing that can help when I'm gone.

They exit.

Scene 11

Song: The Battle of the Sheep!

REGAN: And so to battle again
For this is more than a birthright
I'm holding tight to my reign.

SHADWELL and DANIEL appear.

I'll have them fight till they're dead and slaughtered
And when the battle is done

SHADWELL: We will be safe

REGAN: And when the fighting is over

SHADWELL: Our cause is true

REGAN: I may be standing alone

SHADWELL: So take my hand

REGAN: But I'll be handing my throne to no one
Never

REGAN/SHADWELL: Nothing can prevent what's gonna
happen
here
Nothing can prevent what lies ahead.

REGAN: Nothing matters more to me than when I've won
When I see my sister's army dead

REGAN/SHADWELL: For the fate of Cordelia's in the
hands of a sheep

SHADWELL: And a boy called Daniel.

SHADWELL and DANIEL exit.

CORDELIA enters.

REGAN: And so the sixty-eight fields.

CORDELIA: He will be safe.

REGAN: We paint in shadows of red.

CORDELIA: Our cause is true.

REGAN: We're fleecing sheep as they fall.

CORDELIA: I have no fear.

REGAN: And so to victory near.
Certainly mine!

CORDELIA: Nothing can prevent what's gonna happen
next
Nothing can hold back the rolling stone
Nothing comes of nothing was my father's text.

REGAN exits.

But I know I'll see him safely home
For the fate of Cordelia's in the hands of a sheep
In the boy called Daniel.

SHADWELL: (*Entering.*) And just when things were look-
ing
      over
And just when Regan thought she'd won
A cry was heard: the cry of Shadwell Supersheep.

REGAN enters.

The fight had only just begun

REGAN/SHADWELL/CORDELIA:
Nothing can prevent what's gonna happen now
But no one can be sure who's gonna win
And nothing matters more than what today will bring
When we see which way the flowers fall
For the fate of Cordelia's in the hands of a sheep
And a boy…
Yes a boy…

CORDELIA exits as the rest of the company enter.

SHADWELL: (*Speaks.*) And so it came to pass that the
armies turned their eyes to the strong hands of a boy.
Hands that have held a baby. Hands that have boxed a
wolf.

DANIEL runs on wearing his boxing gloves.

DANIEL: (*Speaks.*) Come and get it sheep.

REGAN: (*Speaks.*) Maaah!

With one punch he knocks her out.

CHORUS: And the fate of Cordelia has been saved by the

hands
Of a boy
Called
Daniel!

DANIEL: The name's Daniel. With a capital Baaah!

SHADWELL: Come on Daniel, we'd better get back to the baby.

DANIEL: Let's go, then!

BOTH: Supersheep to the rescue!

They exit.

Scene 12

Old Red's Cabin.

CORDELIA enters with her father, KING RAM, who holds the flute in his hands.

CORDELIA: It's all right, Father. I'm here now. The baby is safe, too. She'll be taken to her father soon. Where she belongs; just as I belong with you.

KING RAM: Where have I been? Where am I? I don't know what to think. But I think you might be my child, Cordelia.

CORDELIA: I am.

KING RAM: My little lamb. Tell me that you hate me, for I have been unkind to you and I deserve your hate.

Song: The Plan (reprise).

CORDELIA: Father, I never thought I'd lose your love
Father, it breaks my heart to see you suffer
Now
Wherever you have gone
I want you to know you're with me
And you will live simple and free
You and I.

KING RAM: How I love when you sing for me. My little Polly Anna Polly Clogs.

CORDELIA: (*Tending his fleece.*) Polly Anna Polly Clogs? I

remember that story. She was the fisherman's daughter. But he was lost at sea. And, so she pretended she was a fish, a blue fish, that would one day rescue him.

KING RAM: Baah! Blue fish.

CORDELIA: Eventually she was living in a fantasy world, where nothing could harm her. For her world was an ocean of rainbows: full of love, and joy, and music.

KING RAM: I love music.

CORDELIA: Then let me play the flute for you, father. (*She takes the flute from him.*)

RED: (*Entering with EDDIE.*) Where's Shadwell?

CORDELIA: They're at the battle.

RED: But it's all over. What's taking them so long? Eddie, get the baby!

EDDIE: Oooh, oooh!

CORDELIA: Who won the battle?

RED: We did.

CORDELIA: Then what's wrong?

RED: Victoria Red is coming here to kill the baby.

EDDIE comes in with the baby.

CORDELIA: No.

HAGGIS enters, followed by VICTORIA RED holding DANIEL.

VICTORIA: So, Old Red Riding Hood, we meet again.

DANIEL: I'm sorry, Red, I got caught by the harpy.

RED: It's all right, kid. You're not invited here, Victoria. Leave this house at once.

VICTORIA: Oh, why don't you just make me, then? I'm far more powerful than I ever was, old woman. Now, give me the baby, or he'll kill you all!

HAGGIS: Yes, kill them all!

VICTORIA: The baby?

RED: Over my dead body!

VICTORIA: Suit yourself. Haggis, kill them!

RED tries to use magic on VICTORIA, but with one hand VICTORIA throws RED to the floor.

HAGGIS: Now to kill them all!

SHADWELL: (*Offstage.*) Not so fast!

Music is heard.

DANIEL: It's Shadwell!

SHADWELL: (*Running on.*) Supersheep to the rescue!

CORDELIA: Thank heavens.

VICTORIA: Oh, how dreadfully common. Haggis, crush her like a bug.

HAGGIS: Sure thing!

SHADWELL: Look Haggis, look what I've got.

HAGGIS: What?

SHADWELL: Robbie Burns, page 137: 'Address to a Haggis'!

HAGGIS: No! No, please, not that! Anything but that!

SHADWELL holds a book of Robert Burns' poetry, and a knife.

SHADWELL: But mark the Rustic, haggis-fed

The trembling earth resounds his tread
Now, quick, Red, pull the harp string from his stomach!

RED rushes forward and pulls the harp string.

HAGGIS: Please, no! Please stop, I promise to be good.

SHADWELL: And dish them out their bill o' fare
Auld Scotland wants nae skinking ware
That jaups in luggies
Cordelia, pull his middle finger off!

CORDELIA does so.

HAGGIS: I'll even work for you!

SHADWELL: But if ye wish her gratefu' prayer
And this one's for me!

She runs at him and plunges the dagger into him.

Gie her a Haggis!

HAGGIS: (*Running off.*) Noooo!

ALL: Hooray!

SHADWELL: That's all he was made of. The finger of a
naughty boy, a broken harp string, and a haggis.

RED: How did you know?

SHADWELL: A little help from a musician friend of mine.
(*She high-fives with the pianist.*)

VICTORIA: (*To musician.*) You, you're fired!

SHADWELL: I think it's you who'll be looking for another
job, love.

VICTORIA: I don't think so, sheep. Now, give me the
baby or the boy gets it!

RED: Wait. Why do you want to marry the Man of Colours? You don't love him.

VICTORIA: He belongs to me.

RED: But why do you need to kill his baby?

VICTORIA: Because it will remind him of her mother.

RED: Not if you bring her up as your own.

VICTORIA: No.

RED: What if I were to tell you I had the lost mirror of Troy?

VICTORIA: What? The one that belonged to Helen of Troy?

RED: The very one. (*She takes out the mirror.*)

VICTORIA: It's stunning.

RED: It's more than that. Listen. Mirror, Mirror, hear our call. Who is the fairest of them all?

MIRROR: Oh shimmering Scarlet, oh beautiful shade
Victoria Red, your beauty may fade
But up until then, no worry or care
For you are the most beautiful, most radiant, most fair.

VICTORIA: It called me the most beautiful. Give it to me.

RED: On one condition.

VICTORIA: What?

RED: You raise this child as your own. You never harm her, or try to kill her again.

VICTORIA: Are you serious?

RED: Do you want the mirror?

VICTORIA: All right. But only while she is a child. Up until her eighteenth birthday.

RED: You have yourself a deal.

VICTORIA: Now, give me the mirror.

CORDELIA: Let go of the boy first.

VICTORIA: (*Pushing him away.*) There!

DANIEL: Ugh! She's got foul breath!

RED: Give her the mirror, kid. (*He hands her the mirror.*) Good boy. Now get out, we'll take the baby to her father.

VICTORIA: He'll still marry me.

RED: I'm sure. Now get out.

VICTORIA: All right. But one last thing. (*Points to pianist.*) I'm finished with him. (*Turns to CORDELIA.*) I want you to play my exit music.

CORDELIA: Me?

VICTORIA: Yes, you. With that flute.

CORDELIA: Red?

RED: Oh, let her have her exit music.

VICTORIA: Thank you.

CORDELIA: All right. Your exit music. (*She plays the flute.*)

VICTORIA: Remember, it's only the baby I can't harm. (*She exits.*)

RED: What's that supposed to mean?

KING RAM: Baaah! I love it when my daughter plays the flute. I'm so proud.

CORDELIA: Oh, I feel so sick suddenly.

DANIEL: What?

CORDELIA falls to the floor.

KING RAM: Baaah! Baaaaah!

EDDIE: Ooh?

RED: Whose flute is that? (*Sniffing it.*) Poison? Oh no! I've been so foolish.

SHADWELL: What are we going to do?

EDDIE: (*Lifting up CORDELIA's arm. It falls.*) Ooh, ooh.

RED: There's still a pulse, but its weakening fast.

DANIEL: She's not breathing.

KING RAM: No, she's breathing, Polly Anna says she's breathing.

SHADWELL: Red, what are we going to do?

RED: There's only one thing to do. I'm going to take the poison out of her body, and into my own.

SHADWELL: No. You can't do that.

RED: Yes, yes I can. I must. I'm not afraid. I've had a wonderful life.

EDDIE: Oooh, oooh.

DANIEL: But who will look after Baby Snow? When she becomes an adult?

RED: I've a feeling that you will, my darling boy.

SHADWELL: Don't do this, friend. You don't have to do this.

EDDIE: Ooh, ooh.

RED: She's coming back to us.

CORDELIA: (*Waking up.*) I'm alive. I'm alive. You saved my life.

RED: It was nothing. The poison is not meant for fairies.

I'll be fine.

SHADWELL: Oh, Red, what have you done? (*To CORD-ELIA.*) She's spent her whole life devoted to others.

CORDELIA: And from now on, so will I. In honour of what you have done for me, Red. (*Beat.*) Shadwell, I wish to become a Supersheep.

SHADWELL: But King Ram is doolally twist round the bend. Who will look after the sheep in the sixty-eight fields?

RED: Daniel will.

DANIEL: Me? I'm just a boy.

RED: You are a boy who boxes wolves. A boy who stands up for sheep.

KING RAM: (*Spinning CORDELIA round.*) Sheep boy. Baby Boy. Sheep boy. Baby boy.

RED: No, we'll have to call you by a new name: a name for a protector of sheep.

SHADWELL: (*Beat.*) Shepherd.

RED: Yes, shepherd, I like that.

CORDELIA: Are you sure you're all right?

RED: I'm half-fairy, Cordelia; the poison won't affect that half of me. But I am too old now for the human world. And so, Eddie, it's time I went back to the ocean. Will you lead me there, sweet monkey?

EDDIE: Ooh, ooh, ooh.

EDDIE hands the baby to DANIEL.

DANIEL: Goodbye, Red.

SHADWELL: Red, please, there must be a way to…

RED: Shadwell, there is much work to do. You need to make Cordelia a Supersheep. Don't worry about me. I'm going to a place where fairies are safe. But you must think of the future. Come along, Eddie.

He leads her off.

They watch a moment.

Then Cordelia kneels by SHADWELL.

DANIEL looks after KING RAM.

SHADWELL: Repeat after me. For Truth.

CORDELIA: For Truth.

SHADWELL: For Justice.

CORDELIA: For Justice.

SHADWELL: For the Golden Fleece!

CORDELIA: For the Golden Fleece!

SHADWELL: I will fight for peace forever and a day.

CORDELIA: I will fight for peace forever and a day.

RED: (*Singing in the distance.*) Here in my heart
Here in my heart. La la.

The lights fade on a final tableau of SHADWELL knighting CORDELIA.

The End.

Optional Encore:

ALL: Supersheep
Supersheep
For truth

For justice
For the golden fleece
Will fight for peace
Forever and a day
Bleat three times and pray
For Supersheep!

SHADWELL: So the journey will continue,

CORDELIA: For the battle still goes on,

CORDELIA/SHADWELL: And wherever there is darkness

RED/REGAN: You will hear the simple song of Supersheep

ALL: The Supersheep
Bleat three times and pray for Supersheep

HAGGIS: For Supersheep

ALL: Bleat three times and pray for super Sheep!!

WWW.OBERONBOOKS.COM

Follow us on www.twitter.com/@oberonbooks
& www.facebook.com/OberonBooksLondon

Printed in the USA
CPSIA information can be obtained
at www.ICGtesting.com
LVIIW020956171024
794056LV00004B/1169